Anne's glory box

Gloria McKinnon

Contents

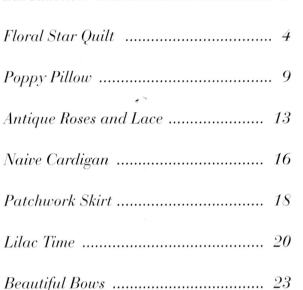

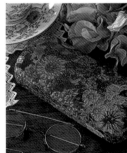

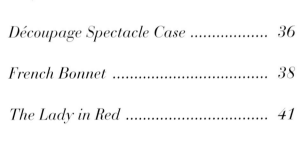

Editorial
Managing Editor: Judy Poulos
Editorial Assistant: Ella Martin
Editorial Coordinator: Margaret Kelly

Photography
Andrew Elton

Styling
Kathy Tripp

Illustrations
Lesley Griffith

Design and Production
Manager: Anna Maguire
Design: Jenny Pace
Layout: Sheridan Packer

Published by J.B. Fairfax Press Pty Limited
80-82 McLachlan Ave
Rushcutters Bay, NSW 2011, Australia
A.C.N. 003 738 430
Formatted by J.B. Fairfax Press Pty Limited
Printed by Toppan Printing Company,
Hong Kong

JBFP 420

ANNE'S GLORY BOX
Series ISBN 1 86343 166 7
Book 8 ISBN 1 86343 251 5

COVER: LLOYD LOOM CHAIR FROM COTSWOLD
FURNITURE, ARTARMON, NSW

From Newcastle to the World

People often ask us, 'Why are you in Newcastle? I wish you were in Sydney or Melbourne'. Newcastle is where we live and, after nearly twenty years at Anne's Glory Box, we are proud to represent our city in both national and international arenas.

Tourism is very important to Newcastle. As we are the starting point for the wonderful wine-growing region in the Hunter Valley, many people come to the area for holidays and for conventions. We are happy to be here to cater for the needleworkers among the visitors to our region. Daily, we meet people in our store from all over Australia and beyond.

Often, people make side trips especially to visit with us; they are then delighted with the beauty of the area and the wonderful beaches that Newcastle has to offer.

A visit to Beaumont Street, Hamilton, brings you to what is now described as 'Eat Street' – a wonderful smorgasbord of cafes and restaurants with cuisines representative of many nations of the world.

Yes, we are truly delighted to be part of the cosmopolitan lifestyle of Newcastle, and to play our part in welcoming visitors to the area.

I hope that we will see you here soon.

Gloria

All the products shown in this book are available from:
Anne's Glory Box
60-62 Beaumont Street,
Hamilton, Newcastle, NSW 2303
Ph: (049) 61 6016 or Fax: (049) 61 6587

Floral Star Quilt

MADE BY BARBARA STEWART

This lovely quilt uses Australian wildflower fabrics designed by Ruth Stoneley.
It is machine-pieced and hand-quilted.

Finished size: approximately 53 cm (21 in) square

Materials

- ♣ 50 cm (20 in) of fabric A, multi-floral
- ♣ 60 cm (24 in) of fabric B, pale yellow
- ♣ 25 cm (10 in) of fabric C, wattle print, for the borders
- ♣ 25 cm (10 in) square of fabric D, striped, for the borders
- ♣ 60 cm (24 in) square of low-loft wadding
- ♣ embroidery cotton: Dusty Mauve, Green
- ♣ Piecemakers crewel needle, size 8
- ♣ quilting thread, Yellow

Method

See the Templates on pages 7-8.

Cutting

1 From fabric A, cut eight triangles using template 1, eight circles 9 cm (3^1/$_2$ in) in diameter for the Suffolk puff flowers, and four strips for the binding, each 8 cm x 55 cm (3^1/$_8$ in x 22 in).

2 From fabric B, cut the backing 60 cm (24 in) square, the centre square using template 2, four corner squares using template 3, and four shapes using template 4.

3 From fabric C, cut four strips, 10 cm x 53 cm (4 in x 21 in) for the borders.

4 From fabric D, cut one heart shape using template 5, and from the green 'leafy' section of the stripe, cut sixteen leaf shapes using template 6.

Piecing

1 Sew the long edge of each triangle to the corresponding edges of the pieces cut from template 4 to form four rectangles.

2 Appliqué the heart to the centre square using blanket stitch and Dusty Mauve cotton.

3 Sew the pieces together to form the star block.

4 Make eight Suffolk puff flowers. Sew the Suffolk puff flowers to the background as indicated on the quilt diagram. Catch them to the background in a random fashion, using French knots in Dusty Mauve cotton.

5 Embroider the flower stems in Green stem stitch.

6 Appliqué the leaves to the background as indicated on the quilt diagram.

7 Sew the wattle-print borders to the four sides, mitring the corners. Press the quilt top well.

Quilting

1 Place the backing face down on a table with the wadding on top and the pieced quilt top on top of that, face upwards. Baste the three layers together securely.

2 Hand-quilt in the borders in your chosen design. Barbara has used simple hearts. Outline-quilt around the star.

Finishing

Fold the binding strips over double with the wrong sides together. Sew the binding on the right side of the quilt with the raw edges matching. Turn the binding to the back of the quilt. Sew the binding to the top and bottom first, then to the sides. Slipstitch all the binding into place.

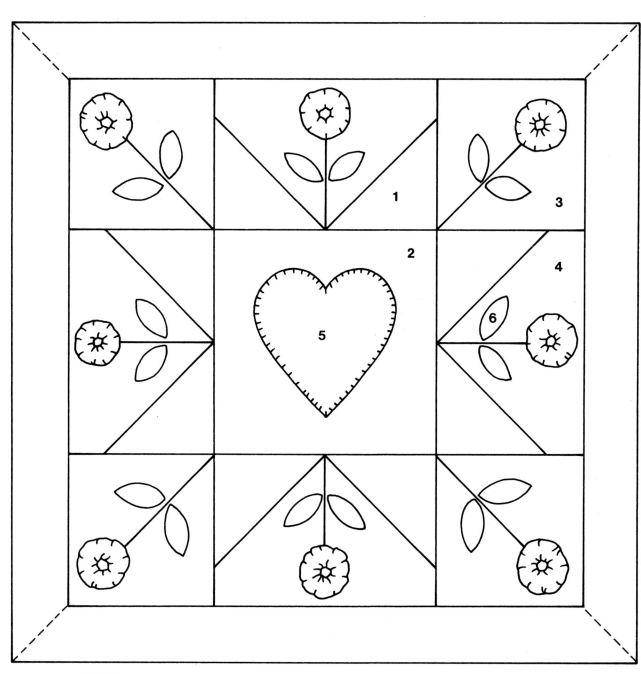

Quilt Diagram

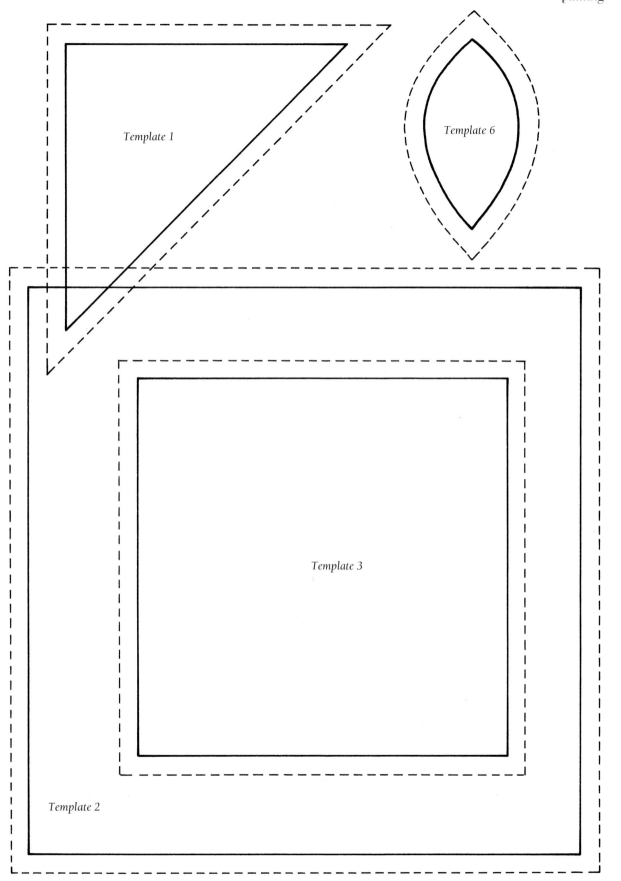

Template 1

Template 6

Template 3

Template 2

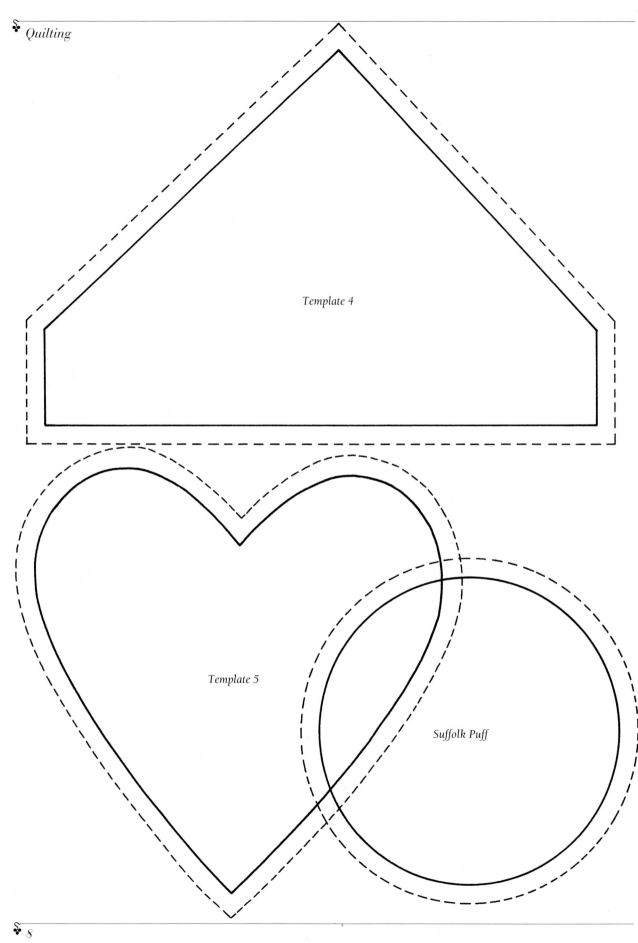

Template 4

Template 5

Suffolk Puff

Poppy Pillow

DESIGNED BY GLORIA McKINNON, STITCHED BY LYN SYLVESTER

These wonderful California poppies add another dimension to silk ribbon embroidery. The overdyed silk bias ribbon is soft and pliable and is ideal for this project.

Materials

- ♣ 1.2 m (1¹/₃ yd) of silk fabric
- ♣ 3.5 m (3³/₄ yd) of 12 mm (¹/₂ in) wide overdyed silk bias ribbon
- ♣ Kanagawa silk twist, Light Olive Green
- ♣ DMC Stranded Cotton to match the silk ribbon
- ♣ Piecemakers crewel needle, size 9
- ♣ 23 cm x 30 cm (9 in x 12 in) of tulle or net
- ♣ 40 cm (16 in) square of Pellon
- ♣ waterproof laundry marker
- ♣ water-soluble marker pen
- ♣ polyester fibre fill

Method

See the Pattern on the Pull Out Pattern Sheet and the Embroidery Design on page 12.

Preparation

1 Cut a 40 cm (16 in) square from the silk fabric. Because the silk frays so readily, it is a good idea to overlock or zigzag the edges. Baste the Pellon to the back of the silk square.

2 Trace the design from the pattern sheet onto the tulle or net using the laundry marker, and allow it to dry completely.

3 Centre the tracing over the square of silk and mark the design onto the fabric using the water-soluble marker. This will leave a series of dots marked on the fabric.

Note: It is always advisable to test the water-soluble marker on a scrap of fabric before you begin.

Embroidery

For the stems and leaves

Complete the embroidery of the stems and leaves before working the flowers. Work the stems and leaf veins in stem stitch, using a small even stitch. Work the leaves in straight stitch, following the outlines to give the shape (Fig. 1). Use the Kanagawa silk twist for all the stems and leaves.

For buds 1 and 2

1 Cut approximately 12 mm (¹/₂ in) of silk ribbon and fold it in half lengthwise (Fig. 2).

2 Fold the ribbon over to form a bud (Fig. 3) then, using one strand of cotton, sew a gathering thread across the base (Fig. 4). Pull up the thread to gather the ribbon, tie off the ends and fold the raw edges to the back. Appliqué the bud into position.

For bud 3

1 Cut approximately 2.5 cm (1 in) of silk ribbon. Fold the ends to the back to make a loop (Fig. 5). Sew a gathering thread across the base. Pull up the thread to gather the ribbon and tie off the ends.

2 Turn the ribbon through so that the gathering is on the inside. Stitch the bud into place. Fix the top of the bud in place with a tiny stitch.

For poppies 1 and 2

1 Cut the remaining ribbon into three lengths. Using a single strand of cotton, sew a gathering thread along one long edge of the ribbon. As you form the poppies, ease the ribbon along this edge as you go.

2 For the first petal, starting at point A, attach the ribbon to the fabric with a small stitch. To begin forming the poppy, fold back approximately 6 mm (¼ in) of ribbon and stitch so that the ruffled edge lies along the line A - B. When you are approaching point B, cut off the ribbon and fold back approximately 6 mm (¼ in) of ribbon as before. Stitch right to point B.

3 Start the second petal just behind the first one, bringing it around to finish at point C (beginning and ending with a fold as before). Now, make the third petal so that it comes in front of the first one.

4 Still using the one strand of cotton, catch the outer edges of these petals approximately 3 mm (⅛ in) from the outer edge at approximately 12 mm (½ in) intervals, ensuring that each small stitch is hidden among the gathers. This will hold the petals on the fabric. You will need to take one row of gathered ribbon across in front of these three petals starting at the base of the third petal and crossing to point C.

5 Embroider the stamens in pistol stitch and French knots. Work the stamens onto the base of the last petal.

6 Work the fourth petal in two parts. Attach a row of gathered ribbon, starting at point D and working back towards point C (with the frill lying across the stamens). Do not cut the ribbon, but work back towards point D with the frill lying away from the centre. When the petal is attached, turn it up toward the centre and catch it as before to hold the petal in position.

For poppy 3

Work as for poppies 1 and 2, except that the fifth petal will lie away from the centre, then a sixth petal will lie towards the centre over the fifth one (as for the last petal on the other flowers). Follow the arrows on the pattern for the direction of the petals.

Fig. 1 Fig. 2 Fig. 3 Fig. 4 Fig. 5 Fig. 6

Finishing

1 Cut four 20 cm (8 in) wide strips across the width of the silk fabric. With the right sides together, stitch the ends to make a loop. Fold the loop over double with the wrong sides together. Overlock or zigzag the raw edges together to reduce fraying. Mark the loop into quarters.

2 Stitch two rows of gathering around the loop and pull up the gathering to fit the pillow. Pin the ruffle to the pillow, matching the quarter marks to the corners, with the frill facing the centre and making sure that all the seams are hidden within the gathers. Stitch the ruffle into place.

3 Cut a 40 cm (16 in) square of silk for the back. Pin the pillow back and front together, with the right sides facing and the ruffle pointing towards the centre. Stitch around three sides and 3 cm (1¼ in) onto the fourth side at each end, taking care not to catch the ruffle into the seam. Turn the pillow to the right side through the opening, making sure that the corners are square. Fill the pillow and slipstitch the opening closed.

Antique Roses and Lace

MADE BY JUDITH COOMBE

This picture will send you on a search through Grandma's wonderful laces or to antique shops in search of old treasures. You may even find a beautiful old frame to use.

Materials

- ♣ printed silk picture
- ♣ piece of Pellon the same size as the picture
- ♣ lengths of antique guipure laces and pieces taken from old laces that have large and interesting flowers
- ♣ 2 m (2¼ yd) each of 12 mm (½ in) wide rayon 'organza look' gold-edged ribbon: Pale Peach, Peach, Deep Pink, Pale Green, Antique Gold
- ♣ five or six small silk flowers (these can be found in antique or second-hand shops)
- ♣ sewing needle
- ♣ sewing thread to match the ribbons

Method

See the Placement Diagram on page 14.

1 Baste the Pellon to the back of the silk picture to give stability to your work.

2 Select four different laces that are suitable for framing your picture and stitch them into position, catching the lace in enough places to hold it securely.

3 Cut the flowers from the pieces of old lace and arrange them over the edges of the picture towards the focal point. Stitch them carefully into position.

For the roses

1 Fold over the end of the ribbon (Fig. 1). Twist the ribbon to make a roll that is quite firm at the base. Stitch the base to hold the roll in place (Fig. 2).

2 For the frilled petals, cut three pieces of ribbon, each 2.5 cm (1 in) long. Fold over the ends and sew a gathering thread across the base (Fig. 3). Pull up the threads to gather the petal (Fig. 4). Attach the frilled petals at the base of the rolled rose (Fig. 5).

For the leaves

For each leaf, cut a 12 mm (½ in) length of ribbon. Fold the edges to the centre to make a leaf shape. Sew a gathering thread across the base. Pull up the thread to gather the ribbon, then wrap the thread around the base. Thread the ends into a needle and stitch through the base to secure (Fig. 6).

Finishing

Attach the roses and leaves in a pleasing trail across the picture. You can even place some small leaves among the laces around the edges.

For the best effect, have your picture framer create a box to give the picture a depth of at least 2.5-4 cm (1-1½ in).

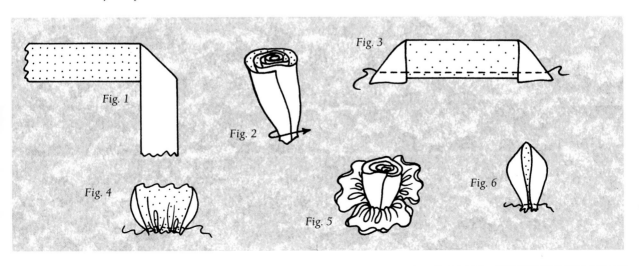

Fig. 1 Fig. 2 Fig. 3 Fig. 4 Fig. 5 Fig. 6

 Wound rose

 Purchased antique flower

 Wound rose with frill

 Leaf

Naive Cardigan

MADE BY DENISE LAWLER

Denise has made a fleecy sweatshirt into a fun 'country' cardigan that is sure to appeal.

Materials

- ❧ lady's or man's fleecy sweatshirt (a man's one is preferable as it is usually longer)
- ❧ piece of fabric that complements the sweatshirt for the bands
- ❧ fabric scraps of your choice
- ❧ iron-on Vilene, medium-weight
- ❧ Vliesofix or Wonder-under
- ❧ embroidery thread or pearl cotton to match the fabric scraps
- ❧ buttons (optional)
- ❧ pencil

Method

See the Appliqué Patterns on the Pull Out Pattern Sheet.

1 Find the centre front of the sweatshirt and carefully cut along the centre line from the bottom of the basque to the top of the neckline.

2 Cut two pieces of fabric, each 7.5 cm (3 in) wide by the length from the top of the neckline to the bottom of the basque. Take care not to stretch the edges of the garment when you are measuring as this will make the bands too full. Do not add a seam allowance.

3 Fold the fabric for the bands in half widthwise so that it is 4 cm (1½ in) wide. Cut a piece of Vilene the same size and iron it on to the wrong side of the bands inside the fold.

4 Fold the bands, with the right sides together, and stitch across the top and bottom ends. Round the top of the bands, if you wish. Turn the bands right sides out. Attach a band to the each front edge of the cardigan, overlocking for a neat finish.

5 Make buttonholes on the right-hand band if you wish to button the cardigan. Sew on the buttons to correspond with the buttonholes.

For the appliqué

1 Trace each part of the design onto the smooth side of the Vliesofix or Wonder-under and cut them out slightly larger than the actual outlines.

2 Choose the appropriate fabrics for the parts and iron the rough side of the Vliesofix or the Wonder-under onto the back of the fabric pieces you have chosen.

3 Cut out the exact shape, peel off the paper and place the shape onto the cardigan. Press with a warm/hot iron to fix the appliqué in place.

Finishing

Using either a blanket stitch or running stitch and three strands of thread or cotton, outline stitch around each part, through all thicknesses.

Note: The instructions for the patchwork skirt are on page 18.

Patchwork Skirt

Made by Fay King

This easy skirt is an ideal casual garment and looks just right with the naive cardigan on page 16. It can be made on your sewing machine or on an overlocker.

One size fits sizes 10-16

Materials

- ♣ 40 cm (16 in) of each of three different 115 cm (45 in) wide fabrics for the skirt body
- ♣ 20 cm (8 in) of fabric for the basque
- ♣ 60 cm (24 in) of fabric for the border
- ♣ sufficient 2 cm (³/4 in) wide waistband elastic
- ♣ matching sewing thread

Method

1 Cut the three skirt body fabrics into twelve pieces, each 20 cm (8 in) wide and half the fabric width long, that is, 57.5 cm (22¹/2 in).

2 Alternating the fabrics, stitch the twelve pieces together into a piece that is twelve strips wide by 57.5 cm (22¹/2 in).

3 Measure around the widest part of the hips and add 2.5 cm (1 in). Cut the skirt basque to this measurement.

4 Using two rows of gathering stitch, gather the pieced skirt body to fit the basque. Sew the skirt body to the basque. Neaten the seam with overlocking or zigzag stitching.

5 Cut the skirt border fabric into three 20 cm (8 in) strips. Join them end to end to form one long strip. Measure and trim the skirt to the desired length, allowing for the addition of the border at the bottom. Sew the border to the bottom of the skirt.

6 Sew the side seam. Neaten the edges of the seam with zigzag stitching or overlocking.

7 Neaten the top edge, then fold it to the wrong side to form a casing 3 cm (1¹/4 in) wide. Stitch the casing, leaving an opening. Thread the elastic through the opening. Adjust the length of the elastic to suit, then join the ends.

8 At the hem, turn up 2 cm (³/4 in), then turn up 2.5 cm (1 in). Stitch and press the hem.

Lilac Time

STITCHED BY GLORIA McKINNON

These pretty boxes come already covered and ready for you to embroider a special lid.

Materials

- ❧ large Sudberry House moiré box
- ❧ 25 cm x 30 cm (10 in x 12 in) of matching moiré fabric
- ❧ 5 m (5½ yd) each of 4 mm (³/₁₆ in) wide silk ribbon: Purple, Deep Lilac, Variegated Lilac
- ❧ Piecemakers tapestry needle, size 22
- ❧ DMC Stranded Cotton, three shades of Green
- ❧ Piecemakers crewel needle, size 8
- ❧ three pieces of Pellon, each 25 cm x 30 cm (10 in x 12 in)
- ❧ water-soluble marker pen
- ❧ craft glue
- ❧ template plastic

Method

See the Embroidery Design on page 22.

Embroidery

1 Using the marker pen, carefully transfer the embroidery design to the centre of the moiré fabric.

2 Embroider the leaves in stem stitch, using one strand of Green, using a different Green for each leaf. Keep the stitches small to make smooth, even lines.

3 Embroider the lilac flowers in ribbon stitch (Fig. 1), working four petals for each flower. The flowers should be quite small and even, so make each stitch 3 mm (¹/₈ in) long. Begin with the main flower at the base, then the intermediate flowers and finally the dark smaller flowers.

Assembling

1 Trace the cardboard lid piece onto the template plastic and cut out the shape. Lay the plastic over the embroidery so that it is centred. Trace around the shape. Trim the fabric so that it extends 2.5 cm (1 in) beyond the traced outline.

2 Cut two pieces of Pellon the same size as the template, and another piece that is 2 cm (³/₄ in) larger all around.

3 Centre the larger piece of Pellon on the cardboard and glue it in place. Clip into the overhanging edges, turn them to the other side and glue them in place. Lay the other two pieces of Pellon on top of the first one.

4 Sew a gathering stitch around the embroidery, approximately 1 cm (³/₈ in) from the edge of the fabric. Place the embroidery on the Pellon-covered piece and pull up the gathering so that the embroidery sits firmly. Lace the back with double threads for strength. Make sure there are no puckers and the edge is quite smooth.

5 Glue the embroidered piece to the pre-made box lid.

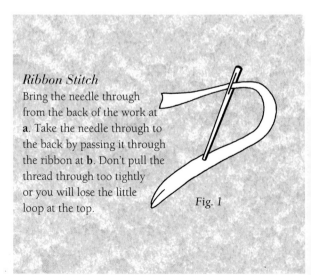

Ribbon Stitch
Bring the needle through from the back of the work at **a**. Take the needle through to the back by passing it through the ribbon at **b**. Don't pull the thread through too tightly or you will lose the little loop at the top.

Fig. 1

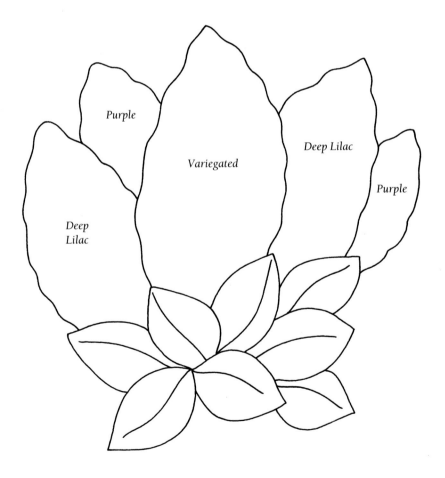

Purple

Deep Lilac

Variegated

Deep Lilac

Purple

*Deep
Lilac*

Beautiful Bows

EMBROIDERED BY WENDY LEE RAGAN

This little pillow is a perfect first project if you are just beginning to work with shadow embroidery.

Materials

- 20 cm (8 in) square of Ulster 14HC white linen
- 20 cm (8 in) square of pink cotton velveteen
- 1.7 m (1⅞ yd) of white Swiss entredeux
- 1.52 m (1⅔ yd) of 7.5 cm (3 in) wide guipure lace
- DMC Stranded Cotton: White, Carnation Ultra Light 818, Carnation Light 3716, Cobalt Blue Light 775, Parrot Green Very Light 472, Jonquil Very Light 3078
- four pink silk ribbon rosettes
- spray starch
- pencil, 2H
- Piecemakers crewel needle, size 8
- cotton fibre fill or wadding
- two 20 cm (8 in) squares of batiste (optional)

Method

See the Embroidery Design on the Pull Out Pattern Sheet.

Embroidery

1 Spray starch and press the square of white linen.

2 Using the pencil very lightly, trace the design from the pattern sheet onto the linen square.

3 Embroider the bows, roses and rosebuds, following the stitch guide on page 24 and using the stitches and colours indicated on the embroidery design.

4 Embroider around the dotted lines between the roses with featherstitching.

Assembling

1 Wash the linen gently in mild soap and allow it to dry naturally. Spray starch and press, as before.

2 Attach entredeux around the edges of the linen and of the velveteen square, using either hand-stitching or machine-stitching.

3 Place the linen and the velveteen together with the wrong sides facing. Join them together around three sides using a whipstitch, stitching through the entredeux.

4 Stuff the pillow or make an inner pillow of the required size from plain batiste and fill that before slipping it into the embroidered cover.

5 Close the fourth side, using a whipstitch.

6 The guipure lace can be attached to the entredeux either by hand or by machine, beginning at one corner. The lace border is straight with mitred corners. As you attach the lace, fold the mitre at the first corner, stitch the mitre carefully, then trim away the excess, before proceeding to the next corner. Repeat until all four sides are trimmed with lace.

7 Attach a ribbon rosette to each corner of the pillow.

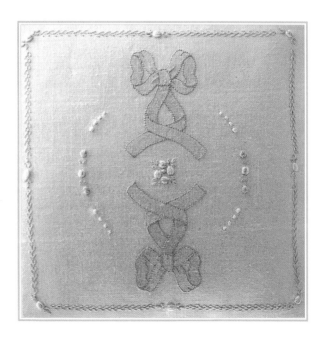

Stitch Guide

Shadow embroidery

Use a crewel needle, size 10, and a 45 cm/18 in single strand of stranded embroidery cotton. Place the fabric in a hoop and begin with a waste knot. In shadow stitch, you form a basketweave of thread that covers the area to be filled and is surrounded by back stitches.

1 Bring the needle through at **a** and take a stitch to **b**. Bring the needle up at **c** and take a stitch to **b**. (Fig. A)

2 Bring the needle up at **d** and take a stitch to **a**. On the wrong side, carry the thread over, bringing it out at **e** and take a stitch to **c**. (Fig. B)

3 On the wrong side, carry the thread over, bringing it out at **f** then take a stitch back to **d**. On the wrong side, carry the thread over, bringing it out at **g** then take a stitch back to **e**. Continue in this way until the area is filled. (Fig. C)

Granitos or rondels

These are tiny dots made by laying six or seven straight stitches over one another. They can be worked with or without a hoop.

Split stitch

This is commonly used for padding which is covered by other stitches. It can be worked with or without a hoop. (Fig. D)

Bullion stitches

Bullion stitches are the basis for many flowers.

1 Begin by anchoring the thread, then take a stitch from **a** to **b**, taking the needle back to **a**. Insert the needle at **b** again, just up to the eye. (Fig. E)

2 Wrap the thread around the needle, keeping it close to **a** (Fig. F). Controlling the wraps firmly with your left thumb, push the needle through and slide the wraps off the needle. Slide the wraps down the thread until they are lying on the fabric. Reinsert the needle at **b**.

Bullion rosebuds are made by laying two bullion stitches side by side. Make one of the bullions one wrap larger than the other.

For a bullion rose, make three bullions side by side. The inside one is usually one or two wraps smaller than the outside ones. Here's a tip: wrap the thread around the needle until the tube is the desired length, then add one more wrap. This is to compensate for the fact that the bullion will compact when you slide it off the needle. For bullion pinwheels, draw a circle of the desired size with a dot in the centre. Stitch around the outside with split stitches, then make bullions from the outside ring, over the split stitches, into the centre, until the circle is filled.

Fig. D

Fig. A

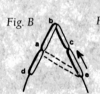

Fig. B

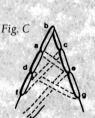

Fig. C

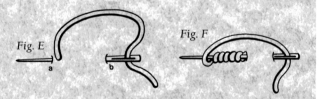

Fig. E

Fig. F

Fay's Garland

EMBROIDERED BY FAY KING

Springtime blooms adorn this pretty garland of flowers tied with an embroidered bow.

Materials

- 80 cm x 115 cm (32 in x 45 in) of wool blanketing
- 140 cm (56 in) of backing fabric
- 4 m (4½ yd) of cream satin piping
- DMC Tapestry Wool: White, 7262, 7192, 7194
- Appleton's Crewel Wool: Blue, Lavender, Deep Mauve, Butter Yellow, Plum, Yellow, Mid-green, Pale Green, Pale Pink, Dark Green, Aqua
- Piecemakers tapestry needle, size 22
- water-soluble marker pen

Method

See the Embroidery Design and the Bow Pattern on the Pull Out Pattern Sheet.

1 Mark a circle with a 35 cm (14 in) diameter on the wool blanketing. You can baste in the circle or use the marker pen. Mark in the bow.

2 Embroider the garland, following the embroidery design and the stitch guide beginning on page 28. Embroider the bow in small stem stitches, using one strand of Aqua.

Finishing

1 Lay the backing fabric face down on a table. Lay the wool blanketing on top of that, face upwards. Make sure the wool is centred on the backing. Baste the two layers together, beginning at the centre and working out to the edges.

2 Trim the backing fabric so that it is 10 cm (4 in) bigger all around than the wool blanketing.

3 Pin the piping to the wool, 5 cm (2 in) from the edge, with the piping towards the centre. Fold the backing fabric over to the edge of the wool, then fold it again to meet the piping. Pin the border in place, folding the corners into mitres. Slipstitch the border into place, stitching through the piping and the wool, but not the backing. Stitch the mitres down.

Stitch Guide

Wool Rose

Use two shades of wool, one light and one dark. With the darker wool, work four straight stitches beside one another. Still using the darker wool, work another four straight stitches over the top of the previous ones.

Using the lighter shade of wool and beginning three-quarters of the way along the side, work four straight stitches diagonally across one corner of the square. The fourth stitch is very small and is almost under the third one.

Continue in this manner, stitching over each corner of the square.

If the rose needs to be rounded out a little, moving clockwise, work small stem stitches around the outside.

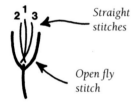

Rose Bud

Using a darker Pink, work three straight stitches, with the outer two crossing over slightly at the base. Work an open fly stitch in Green around the outside of the bud.

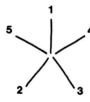

Daisy

Daisy petals should always be worked from the centre outwards, following the order indicated. Work the petals in Butter Yellow.

Stitch each petal, using lazy daisy stitch. When the petals are complete, work a French knot in the centre in Plum.

Rose Leaf

Begin with a straight stitch and then work as many open fly stitches in a single strand of Green as you need to give a nice leaf shape.

Lavender

Baste in a curved line as a guide. Using Appleton's Lavender wool, work five straight stitches together, then four straight stitches, then three, then two, then one.

Forget-me-not

Use these small flowers as fillers. Make each petal as small as possible.

Using two strands of Appleton's Blue wool and following the steps for a five petal flower, work a tiny flower with straight stitches. Work three or four stitches into the same two holes for each petal. Work a French knot in the centre in Butter Yellow.

Lily of the Valley

Using two strands of fine White wool, work four straight stitches on top of one another. Work an open fly stitch in White so that the 'arms' extend beyond the centre stitches. Work a Pale Green French knot at the end of the centre stitches. Work the stems in stem stitch in Pale Green.

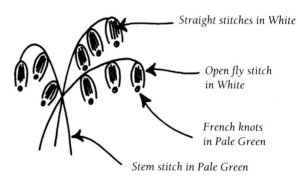

Straight stitches in White

Open fly stitch in White

French knots in Pale Green

Stem stitch in Pale Green

Wisteria

Using the Mushroom wool, work two stitches one on top of the other. Work open fly stitches around the flower centre in Deep Mauve wool.

Work large open leaves in Green lazy daisy stitch and tendrils in Green stem stitch.

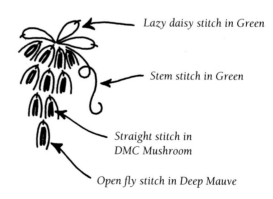

Lazy daisy stitch in Green

Stem stitch in Green

Straight stitch in DMC Mushroom

Open fly stitch in Deep Mauve

Blossoms

Using exactly the same stitches as for the wisteria, work the centres in thick White wool, the fly stitch in fine Pale Pink wool and the leaves and stems in Pale Green.

Violets

Stitch the flower using a single strand of Purple wool. Make two large lazy daisy stitches at the top and three small ones at the bottom. Make a Yellow French knot in the centre.

For the bud, work a very small lazy daisy stitch in Deep Mauve with a Green open fly stitch around it. The stem is a long straight stitch. Work the leaves in Green buttonhole stitch.

Three straight stitches in DMC White

Open fly stitch in Pale Pink

Pale Green lazy daisy stitch

Gloria's tips
for Successful Wool Embroidery

Wool embroidery, like silk ribbon embroidery, is rewarding and forgiving. With a few tips, you can make any one of the beautiful projects in this book.

Threads
Experiment with the variety of woollen threads available. In most cases, you can choose a wool which suits you, the effect you wish to create, and is easily available. Some of the threads you can use are: Appleton's Crewel Wool, Appleton's Tapestry Wool, DMC Tapestry Wool, DMC Medici Wool, Fancyworks Overdyed Wool, Royal Stitch Wool and Kacoonda Threads.

Always use a manageable length of thread. Generally, finger to elbow is the recommended length, but I have to confess, I leave it a little longer. I usually begin stitching with a knot.

Needles
You will need an assortment of needles in sizes from 18 to 24. I like to use Piecemakers tapestry needles, using the ones with larger eyes for tapestry wool and the ones with smaller eyes for crewel wool.

Fabrics
As a general rule, use the best quality fabric you can afford. The blankets in this book have been made using one hundred per cent pure Australian wool This can be handwashed but I also wash blankets in my washing machine on a gentle cycle. Use a good quality wool wash and stay by the machine so you can stop the spin cycle before the blanket becomes felt. Spin only long enough to remove the excess water, then dry it outside on the clothesline.

Transferring a design
In this book, you will find embroidery designs given in detail. There are a number of methods for transferring an embroidery design to your fabric. Using transfer paper is probably the easiest. Simply trace the design from the pattern sheet or page, then transfer it using the transfer paper.

However, don't be too pedantic. This is a form of creative embroidery – so create! Use the pictures as a guide, but don't worry if your flowers are in slightly different positions or are different colours. Embroider them in a way that pleases you.

Log Cabin Quilt

MADE BY FAY KING

The Log Cabin quilt has been a favourite over many years, and was often made from small fabric scraps left from dressmaking and from clothing remnants. This quilt has a real scrap-bag look and is made from many, many different fabrics.

Organise your fabrics into lights and darks, using a colour theme. The lights in this quilt are warm and the darks use a lot of reds and navies. Beyond this, there is no planning of colour. When the fabrics are cut into strips, they are placed into a light pile and a dark pile. The choice of strips for the quilt is random.

This quilt is made stitching strips onto a premarked foundation fabric.

Total number of blocks: 60

Finished size: approximately 128.75 cm x 202.5 cm (51^1/$_2$ in x 81 in)

Materials

- ❦ 2.6 m (2³/₄ yd) of a cream or white evenweave fabric, such as fine lawn, for the foundation
- ❦ light and dark fabrics cut into 4 cm (1¹/₂ in) strips. (If you are buying fabrics, buy 20 cm (8 in) of a number of fabrics)
- ❦ sixty 5 cm (2 in) squares in dark colours for the block centres
- ❦ 2 m (2¹/₄ yd) of fabric for the borders
- ❦ 2.8 m (3¹/₄ yd) of fabric for the backing
- ❦ 2.2 m (2¹/₃ yd) of wadding
- ❦ Pigma pen
- ❦ five hanks of stranded cotton to tie the quilt
- ❦ straw needles

Method

See the Block Foundation Pattern on the Pull Out Pattern Sheet.

Cutting

From the foundation fabric, cut sixty 21.5 cm (8¹/₂ in) squares. Onto these squares, trace the whole log cabin block using the Pigma pen. These lines are your stitching lines.

The marked side of the block will be called the wrong side and the unmarked side will be called the right side. Strips should be attached on the right side around the centre square in an anticlockwise direction.

For the block

1 Pin or baste a 5 cm (2 in) square on the centre of the right side of the foundation fabric with the face up.

2 Lay a light strip face down over the centre. Turn the whole piece to the wrong side and stitch the first line, locking the thread at each end. Turn back to the right side, fold the strip into position and press.

3 The second strip is also light. Lay it face down on the right side in its position. Stitch on the wrong side. Fold the strip back and press as before. Trim the strip to fit.

4 The next two strips are dark. When they are attached as the first two, you will have completed one round. Each new round starts with a light fabric and on the same side as step 1. There are four rounds to complete the block. Make sixty blocks in this way.

Assembling

If the fabrics are randomly selected, there is no need to lay out the blocks in any order. Use the placement diagram below to join the blocks into the quilt top.

Join the blocks by stitching on the outside line of the block, pinning carefully to ensure matching seams. Make ten rows of six blocks each, then join the rows into two sets of five rows. Finally, join the two halves through the centre. When joining the rows, press the seams in alternate directions so that they snuggle together.

For the borders

Cut four long strips, each 10 cm (4 in) wide. Attach the strips to the long sides first, using 6 mm ($^1/_4$ in) seams, then attach the borders to the top and bottom of the quilt top.

Tying

1 Cut and rejoin the backing fabric to fit the quilt top. The join will run across the quilt.

2 Lay the backing fabric face down on a hard surface with the wadding on top, then the quilt top on top of that, face upwards.

3 Baste from the centre to the edges so that the layers are securely held, then baste around the outside edge.

4 Tie the quilt at regular intervals, starting from the centre and working to the edges. Each block should be tied as shown in figure 1. Using the full six strands of the stranded cotton, stitch from the front to the back and to the front again, coming up about 3 mm ($^1/_8$ in) away. Repeat this step. Tie the two ends in a reef knot (right over left, then left over right). Trim the ends to approximately 1 cm ($^3/_8$ in).

Finishing

To finish the edges, turn under a 6 mm ($^1/_4$ in) seam allowance on the border fabric. Trim the wadding to the size of the quilt top. Trim the backing fabric 2.5 cm (1 in) larger. Fold the backing over the wadding (between the wadding and the top) and slipstitch the edges of the top and backing together.

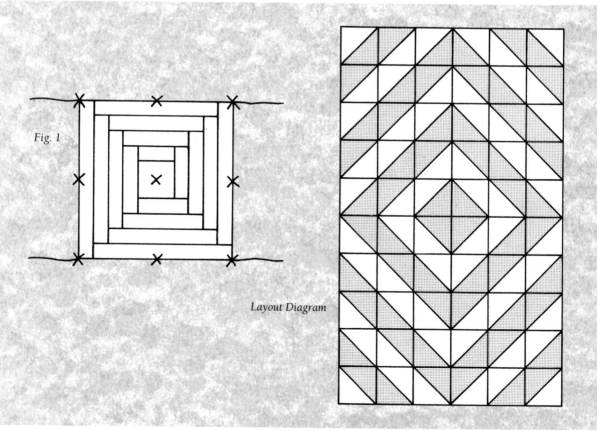

Fig. 1

Layout Diagram

Cosy Cover

Made by Fay King

In winter, there is nothing nicer than resting your feet on a hot-water bottle in a cosy, woolly cover.

Materials

- ❧ 40 cm x 55 cm (16 in x 22 in) of wool blanketing
- ❧ 55 cm (22 in) of Liberty print cotton
- ❧ 50 cm (20 in) of cream satin piping
- ❧ Appleton's Crewel Wool: Pale Peach, Pale Green, White, Yellow, Dark Green
- ❧ Piecemakers tapestry needle, size 22

Method

See the Embroidery Design on the Pull Out Pattern Sheet.

Preparation

1 Cut the wool blanketing into two pieces, each 27.5 cm x 40 cm (11 in x 16 in). Using the curve template provided, shape one short edge of both pieces.

2 On one piece of the wool blanketing, mark the outline of the three topiary trees with a line of basting. Baste in the stems and the outline of the pots.

Embroidery

1 Fill the circle with Pale Peach lazy daisies as shown, following the stitch guide beginning on page 28. Add White forget-me-nots with Yellow French knot centres.

2 Work the filler flowers in small straight stitch stars in Yellow. Work the leaves in detached chain stitches in Pale Green.

3 For the stem, work three rows of stem stitch in Pale Green, alternating the direction of the stitches.

4 Stem stitch the outline of the Versailles pots in Dark Green.

Assembling

1 Stitch the two pieces of wool blanketing together, with the right sides facing, leaving the straight top edge open.

2 Pin the piping cord around the top edge on the right side, so that the piping points away from the opening. Stitch the piping in place.

3 Cut one piece of Liberty fabric, 10 cm (4 in) wide. Stitch the ends together to form a loop. Press the loop over double with the wrong sides together. Sew two rows of gathering around the raw edges of the loop. Pull up the gathering to fit the opening on the cover. Pin, then stitch the ruffle to the cover, stitching in the piping stitching line.

4 Cut two pieces of Liberty fabric the same size as the wool blanketing. Place them together with the right sides facing and stitch around the edge, leaving the top open and a 7.5 cm (3 in) opening in one side. With right sides together, slip the fabric cover over the wool cover. Stitch them together at the top edge, using the same stitching line as before.

5 Turn the cover right side out through the opening in the side seam. Slipstitch the opening closed and push the lining into the wool cover.

For the stars

Take small straight stitches using one strand of Appleton's wool, following the order indicated in figure 1. Add a French knot centre in the same colour.

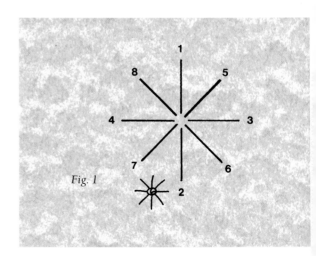

Fig. 1

Découpage Spectacle Case

MADE BY GLORIA McKINNON

Turn a battered old spectacle case or a boring plastic one into an object of beauty that you will be proud to flourish.

We have used Diana Lampe's Embroidered Garden paper, making this an ideal gift for an embroiderer.

Materials

- ♣ very plain hard spectacle case
- ♣ gesso
- ♣ Liquitex Gloss Medium and Varnish
- ♣ small rubber roller
- ♣ small sharp scissors
- ♣ background paper
- ♣ suitable pictures
- ♣ Clag paste
- ♣ Aquadhere PVA glue
- ♣ foam brush, 2.5 cm (1 in)
- ♣ paintbrush, 2.5 cm (1 in)
- ♣ damp cloth
- ♣ Wattyl Estapol, satin finish
- ♣ fine sandpaper
- ♣ steel wool, 0000 grade
- ♣ sepia pencil
- ♣ car polish or furniture wax (optional)
- ♣ lint-free cloth

Method

Preparation

1 Using the foam brush, coat the spectacle case with two coats of gesso. Ensure that the first coat is dry, before adding the second one. Allow the final coat of gesso to dry completely, before proceeding.

2 Using the foam brush again, apply two coats of Liquitex to the spectacle case, allowing each coat to dry before proceeding.

3 Select your pictures. They should be quite small and could follow a single theme. Coat the background paper and all the pictures with one coat of Liquitex.

4 Cut the background paper to fit the spectacle case so that it goes over the lip, but not into the case. For the curved ends, cut darts into the paper, cutting out the excess fullness so the paper will sit smoothly. Take care to cut the darts so the edges meet evenly with little or no overlapping.

Découpage

1 Mix three parts Clag paste to one part Aquadhere until you have a very smooth consistency. Using the foam brush, coat the spectacle case with the glue mixture. Place the background paper on the case and smooth it down. Position the cut ends so they meet neatly. Using the roller, gently work over the case, pushing out any excess glue. Keep wiping the roller to keep it free of glue.

2 Carefully cut out the pictures with the small scissors. Make sure all the edges of the pictures are very neatly cut. If there are any white edges showing, you can colour these with the sepia pencil.

3 Position the pictures on the background paper in a pleasing arrangement before you begin to stick them down. Note that the pictures will come down the sides of the case and over the curved ends. You may need to treat these in the same way as the background paper, cutting small darts to allow them to sit smoothly. Glue the pictures into place, using the roller each time to remove excess glue.

4 When all the pictures are glued down, clean off any excess glue with a damp cloth, then cover the piece with two coats of Liquitex, allowing it to dry completely between coats.

5 Apply twelve to fifteen coats of Estapol, using the paintbrush. Sand vigorously to remove any high points. Continue to add coats of Estapol, sanding again after every two or three coats until you are pleased with the finish.

6 Gently rub over the piece with the steel wool. Add a final coat of Estapol or finish your spectacle case with car polish or furniture wax.

French Bonnet

MADE BY SUSAN D. YORK

This bonnet was made to fit a doll, but you could adjust the measurements to allow it to fit a new baby.

Fits a 46 cm (18 in) doll

Materials

- ✿ **30 cm (12 in) of Swiss organdie or Nelona**
- ✿ **1.37 m (1¹/₂ yd) of insertion lace**
- ✿ **2.75 m (3 yd) of lace edging**
- ✿ **matching sewing thread**
- ✿ **1 m (1¹/₈ yd) of 7 mm (⁵/₁₆ in) wide silk ribbon**

Method

See the Pattern on page 38.

1 Cut a piece of organdie or Nelona, 13 cm x 115 cm (5 in x 45 in) for the back puffy part. Sew two rows of gathering stitches across one long side and gather up the strip as tightly as possible. Using a French seam, sew the short ends together, forming a tube. Tie the ends of the gathering threads together to hold the tube in a tight circle.

2 Cut a piece of organdie or Nelona, 6.5 cm x 115 cm (2¹/₂ in x 45 in), for the main ruffle. Zigzag a piece of lace edging down one 115 cm (45 in) side. Trim the fabric from behind the lace.

Mark the centre of the length of the ruffle. Sew two rows of gathering stitches along the other long side of the ruffle.

3 Cut a piece of organdie or Nelona, 5 cm x 57.5 cm (2 in x 22¹/₂ in) for the front ruffle. Using the curved guide provided below, cut the two front corners of the ruffle (Fig. 1). Attach lace edging to the front (curved) edge of the ruffle. Trim the fabric from behind the lace. Mark the centre of the length of the ruffle. Sew two rows of gathering stitches along the other long side of the ruffle.

4 Cut a piece of organdie or Nelona, 5 cm x 22 cm (2 in x 8¹/₂ in), for the fancy band. Attach insertion lace all around the fancy band, mitring the corners. Trim the fabric from behind the lace. Zigzag down the folds of the mitres, then trim away the excess lace from the corners.

5 Using the crown pattern provided, cut a circle of organdie. Attach insertion lace all around the crown, stitching only the inside thread of the lace. Position the crown in the opening of the tube. Pin, then zigzag it into place. Trim the excess fabric from behind the lace. If you wish, you can join the remaining insertion lace and lace edging to form a wide fancy ruffle. Zigzag the ends together, then attach this ruffle around the circular back of the bonnet.

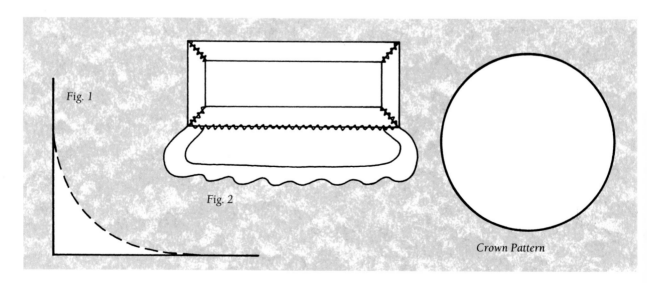

Fig. 1

Fig. 2

Crown Pattern

Assembling

1 Gather the front ruffle to fit the fancy band (Fig. 2). Position the ruffle with the second row of gathering stitches on the edge of the insertion lace on the fancy band. Zigzag the ruffle into place. Trim any excess fabric.

2 Mark the centre of the ungathered side of the tube. Sew two rows of gathering stitches around the tube, starting and finishing 6 cm (2½ in) from the back seam. Gather the tube up to fit the fancy band, matching centre marks. The remaining part of the tube not gathered into the fancy band should measure approximately 13 cm (5 in). Tie off the gathering threads.

3 Mark the centre of the main ruffle. Sew two rows of gathering stitches along one long side. Using a French seam, join the ends. Pin the ruffle to the bonnet front, beginning at the centre front and working down one side first, then the other side. Adjust the gathers so they lie evenly all around.

4 Position the heading thread of the insertion lace of the fancy band so that it lies on the second row of gathering. Pin, then stitch the fancy band in place. The part in the tube which does not have insertion lace, the fabric of the bonnet back and the main ruffle are sewn with a straight stitch along the line of the gathering with the right sides together. Trim away any excess fabric. In the back, zigzag the raw edges together.

5 Attach a length of ribbon to each side of the bonnet front to use as ties.

The Lady in Red

Painted By Kath Connell

A book on medieval art inspired Kath to paint this beautiful glove box, because the elegance and simplicity of the lady in red had such appeal.

Materials

- ❧ Paul Foster glove box
- ❧ Jo Sonja's Artists Colors: Rich Gold, Pale Gold, Brown Earth, Warm White, Napthol Red Light, Cadmium Scarlet, Paynes Gray, Burnt Umber, Yellow Oxide
- ❧ Jo Sonja's Clear Glaze Medium
- ❧ base paint, Black
- ❧ flat brush, 2.5 cm (1 in)
- ❧ dagger brush, 2 cm (³/₄ in)
- ❧ liner brush
- ❧ flat or round brush, 2.5 cm (1 in)
- ❧ sea sponge
- ❧ varnish
- ❧ beeswax (optional)
- ❧ white tracing paper
- ❧ stylus
- ❧ pencil

Method

See the Painting Design on the Pull Out Pattern Sheet.

Preparation

1 Basecoat the sides of the box in at least two coats of Black, sanding between coats.

2 Paint the bottom and the interior of the box in a mixture of equal parts of Cadmium Scarlet and Napthol Red Light. If you do not want such a richly coloured interior, you could use another colour or you could line the box with fabric.

3 Paint the front and back of the lid with two coats of Rich Gold.

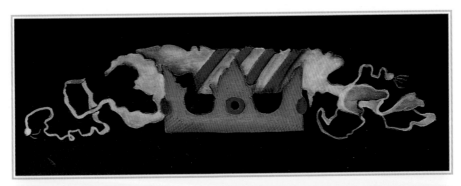

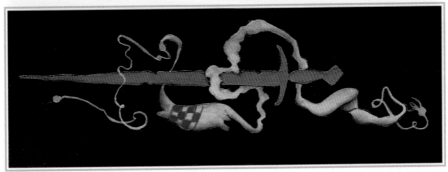

For the design

1 Using the large flat brush, paint the lid of the box with a 3:1 mixture of Brown Earth and Clear Glaze Medium, brushing lengthwise lightly but quickly. Using the damp sponge, pull back some of the colour by sponging very lightly to give an aged look. If this does not work the first time, sponge the lid completely clean and do it again until you have the desired effect. Leave the lid to dry.

2 Transfer the major design lines from the pattern sheet to the lid, using the tracing paper and the stylus. Do not transfer the inner lines of the fabric and the facial features at this time.

3 The gown is a mixture of equal parts of Napthol Red Light and Cadmium Scarlet. Using the flat or round brush, block the gown in, leaving the belt and cloak edging in Rich Gold.

4 The skin is a mixture of Warm White with a touch of Yellow Oxide and a touch of Napthol Red Light. You will not need much, so mix the colours sparingly. Paint on several coats to cover the gold base. When you are painting the fingers, make them long and elegant.

5 Trace the rest of the pattern, the inner lines of the gown and the face and transfer them to the lid of the box, taking care to keep the lines light and precise when you are drawing in the face.

6 Using Paynes Gray, paint in the lines of the gown, making some of the lines heavy and some light, as shown. Using the dagger brush, load the tip and palette blend. Place the tip of the brush on the line and lay down a light shadow. If the gown becomes too dark, load the brush in the Napthol Red Light and put in some highlights on the opposite side to the shadow.

7 Using the dagger brush and Brown Earth with a touch of Napthol Red Light, paint some shadow around the face, under the wimple and the chin. As this is a wash, you will not see the colour on your brush. Add a little more Napthol Red Light and apply it like blusher across the cheeks. The outline is straight Brown Earth, the eyes have a touch of Burnt Umber and the lips are Napthol Red Light. It is important to make the colouring as light as possible. Shade the hands the same colour as the face.

8 Using the dagger brush, highlight the wimple in Pale Gold as shown. This gives the wimple a lovely weightless look that catches the light. Outline the wimple in Brown Earth.

9 The banner with the sword is Warm White, shaded in Brown Earth and Napthol Red Light. The checks are Napthol Red Light. The sword is Rich Gold shaded in Napthol Red Light.

10 The banner with the crown is a wash of Warm White (two coats) to give it a transparent look. It is shaded in Brown Earth and Napthol Red Light. The stripes are Napthol Red Light.

11 The scroll is a series of comma strokes picking up Rich Gold and Pale Gold alternately. The more paint on your brush, the more ornate it becomes. Do not clean the brush between the golds – this gives a lovely range of tones.

12 Finish the box using your favourite varnish. This box has been rubbed with beeswax to give a feeling of warmth and age.

Bridal Album

Embroidered by Gloria McKinnon, covered by Janelle Meston

This photograph album has been lovingly embroidered and covered to hold beautiful memories of a bride's special day.

Materials

- ❧ 75 cm (30 in) of pink Swiss Nelona batiste
- ❧ 10 m (11 yd) each of 4 mm (3/16 in) wide silk ribbon: Pink, Pale Pink
- ❧ cotton thread, Pale Pink
- ❧ DMC Stranded Cotton: Ecru, Pale Green
- ❧ bread dough cherub
- ❧ Piecemakers tapestry needle, size 22
- ❧ Piecemakers crewel needle, size 8
- ❧ glass-headed pin
- ❧ 40 cm (16 in) of Rayfelt
- ❧ 40 cm (16 in) of Pellon
- ❧ 450 Craft Glue
- ❧ spray adhesive
- ❧ refillable photograph album with screws
- ❧ sheet of cardboard, white (ivory-board weight)
- ❧ 15 cm (6 in) embroidery hoop
- ❧ HB pencil
- ❧ Fray Stoppa
- ❧ 1 m (1⅛ yd) of 5 cm (2 in) wide pink organza ribbon

Method

See the Embroidery Design on page 47.

Weaving

1 Measure the front cover of the album and cut a piece of batiste that is 10 cm (4 in) wider and 10 cm (4 in) longer. Using the pencil, trace the heart shape onto the centre of the fabric.

2 Secure the fabric in the embroidery hoop so that the entire heart shape is showing. The woven ribbon pattern on the heart is worked with the Pink ribbon travelling vertically and the Pale Pink ribbon travelling horizontally. Using the Pink ribbon and starting at the left-hand side of the heart, lay straight stitches of ribbon side by side so that each one is exactly beside the preceding one (Fig. 1). Stitch, alternating the direction of the stitches, until the entire heart is covered.

3 Using the Pale Pink ribbon and beginning at the base of the heart, bring the ribbon through from the back and begin to weave under and over the Pink ribbon. As each row is completed, take the ribbon through to the back and bring it out again one ribbon width away, ready to begin the next row of weaving. Continue in this way until the entire heart is woven, taking care that the ribbons lie flat and smooth. Remove the batiste from the embroidery hoop.

4 Cut a piece of Rayfelt the same size as the batiste and baste it to the back of the batiste, around the edges. Return the piece to the embroidery hoop.

5 Using a long piece of the Pink ribbon, bring the ribbon through from the back at the dip in the top of the heart. Thread a second needle with a length of Pink ribbon and using this ribbon work a French knot over the first ribbon, approximately 6 mm (¼ in) away from the point of exit. Allow the first ribbon to twist once, then secure it with another French knot, approximately 12 mm (½ in) from the previous one (Fig. 2). Continue in this way around the outline of the heart, taking the ribbon to the back when you return to the beginning.

Ribbon roses

1 Thread a crewel needle with the cotton thread. These roses are best wound around a pin and stitched to secure them as you go. Fold down one end of the Pink ribbon and lay the pin into position as shown in figure 3.

2 Roll the ribbon around the pin several times for the centre of the rose. Take a few stitches through the base with the cotton thread to secure the centre.

3 Fold the ribbon back and continue to wind the rose in the same direction (Fig. 4). As you pass the folded section, stitch through the base again, then make another fold. Keep folding, winding and stitching until your rose is the desired size, then wrap the thread securely around the base to secure it. Leave a long length of thread to attach the rose to the heart. Trim the ribbon ends. Make approximately twenty-eight roses in Pink and twenty-eight in Pale Pink.

4 Decide where you will place the cherub, then plan the arrangement of roses around the heart. You can refer to the embroidery design as a guide. Attach the roses, using the thread attached to each one.

5 Using two strands of Ecru cotton and a crewel needle, work French knots around the roses.

6 Using one strand of Green cotton and a crewel needle, work small detached chain stitches for the leaves.

7 Using a length of the Pink silk ribbon, tie a bow and attach it to the dip at the top of the heart. Sew three roses over the knot of the bow, then embroider French knots and leaves around the roses.

8 Using the craft glue, attach the cherub to the heart, so that the roses nestle around it.

Cutting the cover

1 Take apart your refillable photo album so that you have three pieces ready to cover – the front and back covers and the centre binding.

2 Cut a second piece of batiste the same size as the embroidered piece to cover the back of the album.

3 Cut two pieces of batiste the same size as the centre binding without a turning allowance.

4 Cut two pieces of cardboard the same size as the inside of the covers and two pieces of batiste the same size plus 2.5 cm (1 in) turning allowance on each side.

5 Trim the Rayfelt attached to the back of the embroidered piece so that it sits neatly on the cover. Cut a second piece of Rayfelt to sit neatly on top of the back cover.

Assembling

1 Using the spray adhesive, evenly spray the outside of the front and back covers as far as the fold (the attachment area). Place the Rayfelt onto the area you have sprayed, smoothing any lumps from the centre out to the edge.

2 Carefully centre the embroidered design on the front cover, taking care not to catch the batiste underneath. Glue the raw edges of the batiste and Rayfelt to the inside of the front cover.

3 Turn the allowance on the outer edge over onto the inside of the cover. Glue the edge in place, using the craft glue. When you glue down the opposite edge, nearest the binding, you must take into account the fold in the attachment area. Position the attachment area as if the album were closed before gluing the fabric over the edge. Take the edge of this fabric over and underneath the cover and glue it down on the edge of the fold line B (Fig. 5). Turn the fabric over twice so that no raw edges are visible.

4 With the point of a pair of scissors, carefully make two holes in the fabric for the screws and finish the holes with fray stopper.

5 Fold over and glue the raw edges of the top and bottom. Fold the turning allowance over twice so that no raw edges are visible and mitre the corners which fall on the edge of the first side.

6 Cut two pieces of Pellon the same size as the lining cardboard. Using a light spray of glue, attach the Pellon to the cardboard. Smooth out any lumps from the centre to the edge. Trim the Pellon to the edge of the cardboard. Place the Pellon face down on the batiste and glue the raw edges of the batiste over the cardboard, keeping the batiste taut and mitring the corners.

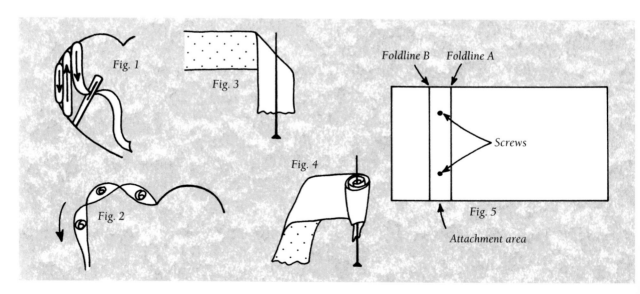

Fig. 1

Fig. 2

Fig. 3

Fig. 4

Foldline B   Foldline A

Screws

Fig. 5

Attachment area

Finishing

1 Cut the length of the organza ribbon in half and, using the craft glue, attach it to the centre of the inside front and back covers of the opening edge to make a ribbon tie. Cut the raw edge of the ribbon on the diagonal and finish the ends with fray stopper.

2 Run a line of the craft glue around the edges of the wrong side of the lining and around the centre and place the lining on the inside covers of the album, pressing firmly for a short time to hold it in place.

3 To cover the centre binding, turn it to the wrong side. This covering should be kept as thin as possible, and so will not require any Pellon or Rayfelt.

4 Lightly spray the white side of the centre binding with glue and cover it with a piece of the batiste, smoothing any lumps from the centre out to the edge. Repeat for the other side.

5 Trim away any excess fabric back to the edge of the binding and cut away any of the fabric which covers the screw holes. Finish all raw edges with fray stopper.

6 Reassemble the photograph album and tie a beautiful bow with the ribbon to close the album.

Template

Embroidery Design

    Leaf

    French knot

    Pink rose

    Pale pink rose